32.04

D1130764

Scat the
Fat Cat

Mary Elizabeth Salzmann

Consulting Editor, Diane Craig, M.A./Reading Specialist

ABDO
Publishing Company

Published by ABDO Publishing Company, 4940 Viking Drive, Edina, Minnesota 55435.

Printed in the United States.

Credits
Edited by: Pam Price
Curriculum Coordinator: Nancy Tuminelly
Cover and Interior Design and Production: Mighty Media
Photo Credits: AbleStock, Digital Vision, Photodisc

Library of Congress Cataloging-in-Publication Data

Salzmann, Mary Elizabeth, 1968-
     Scat the fat cat / Mary Elizabeth Salzmann.
        p. cm. -- (First rhymes)
     Includes index.
     ISBN 1-59679-519-0 (hardcover)
     ISBN 1-59679-520-4 (paperback)
        1. English language--Rhyme--Juvenile literature. I. Title. II. Series.
     PE1517.S3575 2005
     808.1--dc22

                                                                2005048040

SandCastle™ books are created by a professional team of educators, reading specialists, and content developers around five essential components that include phonemic awareness, phonics, vocabulary, text comprehension, and fluency. All books are written, reviewed, and leveled for guided reading and early intervention reading, and designed for use in shared, guided, and independent reading and writing activities to support a balanced approach to literacy instruction.

Let Us Know

After reading the book, SandCastle would like you to tell us your stories about reading. What is your favorite page? Was there something hard that you needed help with? Share the ups and downs of learning to read. We want to hear from you! To get posted on the ABDO Publishing Company Web site, send us e-mail at:

sandcastle@abdopub.com

SandCastle Level: Beginning

AUG 24 2006

-at

bat

cat

hat

mat

rat

Look at the .

Look at the  .

Look at the .

Look at the  .

Look at the .

The bat is big.

The cat is fat.

The hat is green.

The mat is flat.

The rat is white.

Scat the Fat Cat

Scat was a fat cat.

Scat the fat cat
sat on a mat.

Scat the fat cat
wore a green hat
while he sat
on the mat.

Scat the fat cat
put the green hat
on a white rat
who walked
by the mat.

The green hat
did not fit the rat.

From his mat,
Scat the fat cat
saw the rat use a bat
to make the hat flat!

About SandCastle™

A professional team of educators, reading specialists, and content developers created the SandCastle™ series to support young readers as they develop reading skills and strategies and increase their general knowledge. The SandCastle™ series has four levels that correspond to early literacy development in young children. The levels are provided to help teachers and parents select the appropriate books for young readers.

Emerging Readers
(no flags)

Beginning Readers
(1 flag)

Transitional Readers
(2 flags)

Fluent Readers
(3 flags)

These levels are meant only as a guide. All levels are subject to change.

To see a complete list of SandCastle™ books and other nonfiction titles from ABDO Publishing Company, visit **www.abdopub.com** or contact us at:
4940 Viking Drive, Edina, Minnesota 55435 • 1-800-800-1312 • fax: 1-952-831-1632